Introc

The Spirit of the
because God h.
to bring Good News to the poor.
God has sent me to proclaim release to prisoners,
and recovery of sight to the blind,
to let the oppressed go free,
to proclaim the year of the Lord's favor.

(Luke 4:18–19)

We are one year closer to the year 2000, the year of the Great Jubilee when we will commemorate how Jesus came into this world about two millennia ago. From his first encyclical in 1979, Pope John Paul has been suggesting that we should prepare ourselves for this anniversary, and he developed a five-year plan.

This Advent we start the next-to-last year of preparation. In the pope's plan, the year 1998 should be dedicated to the Holy Spirit, who is present in all of us, building God's kingdom among us. The Holy Spirit is also preparing the full manifestation of Jesus Christ, stirring our hearts, and "quickening the seeds of the full salvation that will come at the end of time." The pope reminds us that "the whole of creation, and we, too, groan inwardly, waiting for the coming of the kingdom of God."

The Holy Father is very practical when it comes to seeing how the Spirit is at work in our world. He mentions the scientific, technological, and especially medical progress in the service of human life; the greater environmental awareness; the peace and justice efforts; the global desire for reconciliation and solidarity, especially in relations between the rich north and the poor south. He calls all of these "signs of hope." It is in this context that he asks us to pay greater attention to the voice of the Spirit in ourselves, accepting that we are gifts for one another.

It is in this same spirit that these Advent meditations were written. Based on the Advent liturgical readings, their purpose is to quicken our hearts in a practical and do-able way. I invite you to first read the biblical text for each day. Then spend time reading and reflecting on the meditation. This is followed by a prayer, inspired by the morning and evening prayers in the Divine Office. Finally I offer a sometimes radical "Practice" to crown the prayers and meditations.

May the Spirit of the Lord be upon you throughout the entire Advent season as you prepare for Jubilee Year 2000.

FIRST SUNDAY OF ADVENT

Jeremiah 33:14–16; Psalm 25:4–5, 8–9, 10, 14; 1 Thessalonians 3:12–4:2;
Luke 21:25–28, 34–36

End of Time Perspective

"There will be signs in the sun, the moon, and the stars" (Lk 21:25).

The first gospel reading in Advent sounds threatening. It is about signs in the sky, about light that darkens, powers that are shaken, and the roaring of water. It is about the end of time, and Jesus offers us an "end of time" perspective.

But consider this: at the end of its time, a seed breaks open; a caterpillar turns into a butterfly; a womb painfully opens and a new child is born. What appears to be the end is really a new beginning.

Paul wrote to the Romans that the whole world is groaning for a new beginning. And he adds that we, too, are in the awesome birth pangs of God's renewed creation. We should not only be groaning about the present and being hopeful for the future, we should also be on our watch, aware that we are engaged in the process of giving birth to a new world.

Whether we like it or not, whether we are aware of it or not, every single decision we make, every step we take either eases the birthgiving or slows it. It either helps to close the old and open the new, or to continue the old and delay the new. As Jesus would put it, we are either with him or against him.

Prayer Loving God, let me stand ready and watchful this day. Help me to see my words and deeds, my joys and sorrows, and all my relationships with others as helping the new to come and the old to fade. Amen.

Practice Contribute today to the building of God's new creation, introduced by the birth of Jesus Christ, with an act of kindness to someone you otherwise would have overlooked.

Final Get-together

"Let us go to God's house" (Ps 122: 1).

Today's psalm sings about the final outcome of our human history. God will be a canopy, a tent, a shade, a refuge, and a shelter for all. In the gospel Jesus, too, speaks in these terms. But he turns the scene into a feast, the final feast, the great everlasting get-together of the whole human family, and he is at its center.

This get-together started at the birth of Jesus. Think of the stories that surround this event. God broke the news by sending angels to alert the shepherds nearby, and by lighting a star to attract people from afar. The family from Nazareth was exposed to sights and sounds they had never known in Joseph's carpenter shop: the visit of shepherds and their sheep; the gifts of spices, incense, and perfume; and the look of camels and kings who had traveled a long way.

It was the beginning of a gathering around Jesus that was foreseen by the prophets, a rally that never stopped. According to the Gospel of John, it even has to do with Jesus' death on the cross. He wrote that Jesus was going to give his life "to gather into one the scattered children of God" (Jn 11:52). If that was a reason he was willing to die, it should be a reason for us to do our part in bringing together the whole human family.

Prayer Jesus, you love every human being as you love me. Help me to re-create the earth, and to have an unfailing gentleness for all those I meet along the way. Amen.

Practice Ask advice from someone today who is obviously not of your ethnic group or culture, perhaps advice as simple as directions to the post office or some other nearby place. Just make contact and do some bonding in our scattered world.

Isaiah 11:1–10; Psalm 72:1, 7–8, 12–13, 17; Luke 10:21–24

On Seeing Anew

"Happy the eyes that see what you see" (Lk 10:23).

We had been walking for quite some time. We were deep in a dense forest when my friend asked me to look at the color of the trees. It was the first time that I really looked up at them. And then I saw the amazing variety of colors and ever-changing shades. I hadn't noticed them, though they were there all along. My friend helped me to see; he gave sight to someone who was "blind."

There are so many things we never see, though they are right before our eyes. Jesus helped people to see. The women and men who came to him had been living their daily lives without noticing the resplendent dawn or the evening sky, the lilies of the field, or the birds of the air. It was in his company that they began to notice. Jesus also gave them new insights into themselves, in the people they met, and in the world they thought they knew so well.

Jesus helps us to see as well. He helps us to notice where God's Spirit is at work, for example: in our growing environmental awareness; in peace and justice efforts all over the world; in the global desire for reconciliation and solidarity; and in the scientific, technical, and especially medical progress in the service of human life. When we look through the eyes of Jesus, we begin to understand our call to make the world a better place. "Happy the eyes that see what you see!"

Prayer Almighty God, in whom we live and move and have our being, may we see you in the reality of our world, and may we come to understand what you want us to do. Amen.

Practice Where can you see God's Spirit at work in your life? If you live in a family or a community, try to answer this question not only for yourself but also for one another.

They Have Nothing to Eat

"I don't want to send them away hungry" (Mt 15:32.

When Isaiah describes the world he is very somber. It is, he writes, as if a dark veil is thrown over all people, a web cast over the nations. The world is stuck in the dark, and it cannot wrestle itself free. It is not a nice picture. The world is in a shameful state. Yet, in a way, it is this somberness that gives Isaiah hope. God cannot leave us like this. People today ask the question, "How can God want famine and hunger in this world?" The answer is that God does not want these things. That is why Isaiah was so sure that a new child was going to be born among us, a savior who would show us the way

Jesus is this savior. Today's gospel says that when he looked at the hungry crowd, he felt sorry for all those people. They had nothing to eat, and he did not want to send them away hungry. Jesus gave them the food they needed, using a few loaves and fishes. But he worked *through* his disciples who distributed the food to the crowd.

Liam Hickey, an Irish priest, tells this story: "A young man was angry with God because of all the hunger and famine in the world. That night he had a dream. God spoke to him and said: "I have done great things for the poor and hungry." The young man said, "Like what?" God said, "I sent you!"

Prayer Merciful God, help us to look kindly upon all those who are hungry in our world, and assist us to find ways to enable all to earn and have their daily bread. Amen.

Practice This week farm out a chore that you usually do yourself to someone who needs a job, for example: washing your car, doing your laundry, or mowing the lawn.

The Real Test

"Open to me the gates to holiness" (Ps 118:19).

The talk that evening had been interesting. The speaker was asking for help with a major project. Everyone present must have understood that. Yet, the applause after the presentation had been long and intense. Some had tears in their eyes. When the applause ended the speaker asked for volunteers. This was the real test. "It is not those who talk, but those who are prepared to do God's will, who will enter God's kingdom."

When threatened by a mugger or a thief, people often begin to talk to protect and defend themselves. They think that as long as they can keep a conversation going, nothing will happen to them. Sometimes it works. Many of us seem to follow the same kind of logic in our relations with God. As long as we talk, nothing is going to happen to us. Keep talking and nothing will be asked.

Jesus exposes this strategy in today's gospel. It is not those who say a lot of prayers who are entering God's realm. Rather, "everyone who hears these words of mine and acts on them" will enter God's kingdom. Psalm 118 suggests that those who pray "Open to me the gates of holiness," must be willing to enter those gates!

Prayer Christ Jesus, you who came among us as one of us, transform us into sons and daughters of God. Give us the courage to live as we know we should be living. Amen.

Practice Before you go to bed tonight, kneel down and dare to pray that you want to do God's will. Don't do this in an abstract and general way, but think about what this might mean in practical terms.

On Not Seeing

"I am sure I will see the Lord's goodness" (Ps 27:13).

The two who followed Jesus shouted that they could not see. They followed him to the front door of the house where he was staying. It was then that he turned to them. Again they told him that they could not see. He touched their eyes, and their sight returned. Those two were helpless and in need. They trusted Jesus, not because they had something to offer, but because they knew about his goodness. At the other extreme, we often think that it is our prayers and good deeds that make us lovable in God's eyes. God loves us in weakness, failure, warts, blindness, and all. It is always God's own loving kindness that takes the initiative.

This is the kind of love that is sometimes mirrored in our own human love. Once when I visited a prison in Kenya, the guards told me that many of the criminals were visited regularly by their mothers, sometimes for years on end. When I asked why, they told me: "Mothers say: whatever my child did, he or she remains my child."

It is good to remember this. We are on very shaky ground if we think that our deeds are the reason God loves us. We are often blind to the real reason. It has nothing to do with what we offer God; it has everything to do with God's unconditional love. This is why the one who prayed Psalm 27 was so sure that he would live in the house of the Lord and savor the sweetness of God.

Prayer Almighty God, make yourself known to those who do not see, and take pity on those who struggle and can't find their way. Strengthen me that I might help them to "see." Amen.

Practice Call someone today who is lonely or afraid, someone who would love to hear from you. If he or she asks why you have called, simply answer, "because I love you!"

Isaiah 30:19–21, 23–26; Psalm 147:1–6; Matthew 9:35–10:1, 6–8

Give without Charging

"You received without charge, give without charge" (Mt 10:8).

The family arrived very late in a foreign country, and they were very hungry, so hungry that they probably wouldn't be able to sleep. The hotel restaurant was closed. They would have to find food elsewhere, they were told. Stopping a taxi, they asked to be taken to a restaurant.

The cab driver told them that everything was closed so late in the evening. Then he added: "I know one place, the best in town." They got in the cab, and they were very surprised when they did not stop at a restaurant but at a house. It was the home of the driver, who together with his wife prepared a meal that was—considering the circumstances—terrific.

The driver then took the family back to their hotel. They had to pay for the ride, but the rest was free! When they told the story, they said: "Now we know what the eucharist is all about!"

A dream world? No, this really did happen. And things like this happen all the time! The world depends on those small gifts we give one another! Jesus would smile and say: "You received without charge, give without charge!"

Prayer Let us pray with a joyful heart: Jesus be born among us. Let your Spirit be born and reborn again and again in us and in all those who inhabit our world. Amen.

Practice Today render at least one service just for free, even it it costs you something. Do it for someone who would least expect you to do so. Just say, "You don't owe me anything. It's free."

A Voice in the Wilderness

*"The Word of God came to John,
son of Zechariah, in the wilderness" (Lk 3:2).*

The man bought a new gadget. When he unpacked it he read the slip that advised him to study the manual carefully. He ignored that advice and just started to use it his way. In no time he was frustrated and the gadget was messed up. Most of us have had this experience at one time or another.

This is, in a way, the experience of the human family. When the world was given to us it was very good. "God looked upon all creation, and indeed it was very good" (Gen 1:31). But the new owners wanted to decide what was good and what was bad. They thought they did not need God or God's advice. The world turned into a wilderness.

Thank God that in that wilderness the Word of God could still be heard! It was John the Baptist who heard that voice, and it was speaking of restoration, the filling of holes, straightening, leveling, pruning and weeding, liberation and salvation, repentance and forgiveness, a new life and a new spirit. And the sky and the earth, the water and the air, the fire and the light, the oils and the minerals, the flowers and trees, the animals and their young, and all men and women everywhere, all were once again bathed in hope and joy.

PRAYER Almighty God, help us to play our role in the reshaping of our world. May it once again enjoy the splendor you gave it in the beginning. Amen.

PRACTICE When you are challenged today with a suggestion to be more careful about yourself or your environment, comply without protest.

Grace in Action

"Seeing their faith Jesus said…'Get up'" (Lk 5:20, 24).

Many of us are upset about the world we live in. The news is more often than not very bad. It's so bad in fact that the newscasters often leave the one good story until the end. Without such a story the news would be intolerable. It would paralyze us.

The gospel story today is one of those good stories, and it is filled with hope. It is the story about a paralyzed person who cannot help himself. Alone he can do nothing, but he has some very good friends. When they hear about Jesus being in the neighborhood, they think of the paralyzed man. They take his stretcher, and instead of going through the door into the crowd, they go up to the roof, remove some tiles, and lower their friend in front of Jesus.

A case of grace in action! When Jesus notices their faith, he immediately takes action and unbinds and heals their paralyzed friend. He tells the man that he can get up and go home on his own. And the man does just that. So do his friends, strengthened in the spirit that made them bring their friend to Jesus in the first place!

Prayer Come, Lord Jesus, may the world know the love you proclaimed and lived among us. May your reign come and your glory fill the earth. Amen.

Practice If you meet anyone today who needs a word of hope, take the time to give her or him that word, knowing that the comfort you give will be supported by God's love.

The Greater Joy

"Will he not leave the ninety-nine in search of the stray?" (Mt 18:12).

Jesus' story about the good shepherd is about God and God's love for each of us. It is also a story about Jesus himself; and it is quite an extraordinary story. It is a tale about a certain preference, a predilection for compassion and forgiveness.

Someone told me another story that parallels what happens in the good shepherd story. An old Rabbi had two sons. One behaved well and was the pride of his parents. The second one was a disgrace and ended up badly. When the Rabbi did all that he could to help the second son out of his misery, someone asked him why he bothered. After all, this was his stray son. "Shouldn't you be more interested in your successful son?" He answered: "My stray boy needs my love even more than the other one."

This is the lesson Jesus would like us to draw from his tale about the good shepherd. That shepherd leaves the rest of his flock to look for the one who has strayed. It is this kind of love that Jesus wants us to share with one another. This kind of love is compassionate and forgiving, and it should be our first priority in life.

Prayer Christ Jesus, fill our hearts with your love. Make us long to be united with you, and grant us the strength and courage to serve those who seek your love and forgiveness. Amen.

Practice If you were to take the Good Shepherd story as your model, how would your life change? Think about this today and reach out to someone who has "strayed."

Overcoming Stress

"I will give you rest…" (Mt 11:28).

Studies on stress abound. Just now as I quickly scanned the internet, I found no fewer than 402,574 references to it. Stress is referred to as the new epidemic, and it is affecting more and more lives. Stress is not a completely new phenomenon, however. It existed in Jesus' time. He spoke about it, and he told us what to do about it. He told us to live as he lived, and he added "My yoke is easy and my burden is light."

How was it possible that he called his yoke easy and his burden light, surrounded as he was by people who plotted his death and by friends who betrayed him?

Jesus was speaking about his self-awareness, about his relationship with God, and about having the gentle and humble heart he had. He was able to relax and to cope because he believed that his Father in heaven would always give him the strength he needed. Jesus lived what the prophet Isaiah wrote: "Those who hope in God renew their strength; they put on wings like eagles" (Is 40:31).

Prayer Jesus Christ our Lord, you who came to us as one like us, set free in us what is harmed by sin. Help us to live in imitation of you, ever trusting in God's love. Amen.

Practice Set aside a definite time today for resting in God. Try to enter into yourself, focusing on God's presence in your life and work. Just sit quietly with this awareness, letting it fill your heart, mind, and being.

God Loves the Poor

"The poor and needy…I, the Lord, will not abandon them" (Is 41:17).

If you look through the Bible to find evidence of God's concern for the poor, you will discover that ours is a compassionate God. God provides for the poor (Ps 68:10), delivers the poor (Ps 72:12), secures justice for the poor (Ps 140:12), hears the poor (Job 34:28), does not discriminate against the poor (Job 34:19), protects the poor (Ps 12:5), will not forsake the poor (Is 41:17), and gives food to the poor (Ps 146:7). We read in the prophet Jeremiah that King Josiah "defended the cause of the poor and needy…," and the prophet adds—speaking for God—"Is that not what it means to know me?"

In the gospel Jesus says, "Blessed are the poor in spirit, for theirs is the kingdom of heaven" (Mt 5:3). He also says, "Give to everyone in need, and do not refuse them" (Mt 5:42). If this is the God we serve, we should enter into the spirit of comforting and serving those in poverty.

Being kind to the poor is equivalent to lending to the Lord (Prov 19:17). At the end of his gospel Matthew tells us about the last and final judgment. The judge will be Jesus telling us that he always identified himself with those in need. "Whatever you did for these least ones, you did for me" (Mt 25:40). A rather unsettling picture, when you come to think of it.

Prayer Dear Jesus, do not let us become estranged from you. Keep us from denying you in our actions, and help us to do our part to remove every sorrow from the face of the earth. Amen.

Practice Helping the poor means more than giving alms. It also demands the kind of political action that assists them in a more lasting way. This week find out how your parish helps the poor, and get involved in this ministry, at least in some small way.

A Teaching God

"I, your God, will teach you what is good for you!" (Is 48:17).

They had an accident on the road. One of their children sprained his ankle rather badly. Once they got home they talked about the accident and wondered what God was trying to tell them. They thought that God was teaching them something in particular.

This view assumes that God is always arranging the events in our lives in order to instruct us. God has a lesson plan for us, takes us through learning exercises, and puts us into special circumstances to test and teach us.

It is a common belief, and I often hear it expressed. Yet, it seems to be a risky one. It blesses God when all goes well, but it blames God when the lessons are too hard and seem to be unfair. It puts the burden for the things that happen to us, and for which we are sometimes responsible, on God's shoulders.

We are indeed responsible for our actions. God made this clear in giving us the ten words of life called the ten commandments, and when showing us in Jesus how to live our lives, doing harm neither to ourselves nor to others.

Prayer Almighty God, most merciful, be with us as we prepare to celebrate anew the presence of your son in our lives. Keep us from denying him in our words and actions. Amen.

Practice Check yourself today when you are blaming circumstances, others, or even God for something that is happening to you. Can you honestly say that you are not to blame?

Repair of the World

"Everything is once more as it should be" (Mt 17:11).

In his letter on the Jubilee Year 2000, Pope John Paul II suggests that we should renew our appreciation of the virtue of hope. "This will encourage us," he wrote, "not to lose sight of the final goal that gives meaning to our life and offers solid and profound reasons to transform the world. We should renew our hope in the definitive coming of the kingdom of God, working at it in our own unique context and time."

We should live in our world as a kind of vanguard in view of the final restoration to come. During Advent we are called to renew our commitment to this by reflecting on our place in this world, a world that sometimes seems worn and tarnished and at other times so new. We are also called to renew our faith that "the Holy Spirit will teach us all things, and will help us to remember all that Jesus has said to us" (cf. Jn 14:26).

Driving our cars, sitting in a train, bus, or plane, doing our work, educating the young, we should feel—at least now and then—as aliens, as visitors from the future, guests from God's reign to come.

Prayer God, be merciful to our world which so badly needs restoration. To those who are hungry give bread, and to those who have bread give the hunger for justice. Amen.

Practice To remind yourself of the task to "restore" the world, take care of a repair you have postponed, or weed your garden or unclog a drain. Better yet, help an elderly acquaintance with such a repair.

Zephaniah 3:14–18; Isaiah 12:2–3, 4, 5–6; Philippians 4:4–7; Luke 3:10–18

Sharing the Good News

"...announce the Good News to them" (Lk 3:18).

We are so accustomed to putting the words "Good News" in a spiritualized context, that we often do not even care to find out what the term really meant when the gospels were written. If you do care, you will discover that they refer to an old Roman political slogan. The Roman emperors of that time used the term to proclaim and advertise the "new order" they were promising to realize during their reign.

This is just what our political parties and their candidates promise to do when they are campaigning. All will be new. The old corrupt regime is over. A new era is at hand.

In Luke's text, dishonest tax collectors and rowdy soldiers are asked to change their ways. Those who have more than one tunic are asked to share with those who have none, and those who have more than enough to eat have to do the same with their food.

The Good News promised when Jesus entered our human history is far from a merely sentimental or emotional issue. Axes and winnowing hooks will be used to clear the way. Dead wood and chaff will be burnt.

Prayer Almighty and gracious God, help us to think of the needs of others. We ask the same for our political and business leaders; help them to look beyond their own nations or businesses, to discover how to share the good news your son announced to all. Amen.

Practice Go through your wardrobe and take everything you have not worn in the past year—or at least some of it—to a goodwill or charity shop.

Numbers 24:2–7, 15–17; Psalm 25:4–9; Matthew 21:23–27

In Need of Mercy

*"Remember your mercy, Lord,
and the love you have shown as of old" (Ps 25:6).*

All of us need God's mercy, especially at the last and final judgment. Just picture the scene! You are standing there with people you have known during your life. Next to you is someone who did something to you that you have neither forgotten nor forgiven.

He or she is going to be judged before you. You are listening to the verdict, knowing that you are the next one in line for judgment. Wouldn't it be a relief to you to hear that your archenemy is forgiven? Wouldn't you be afraid for your own lot if God failed to show mercy to the one who offended you?

Forgiveness is the only way to undo the past. It does not mean that we should not recognize our failings. Pope John Paul II wrote in his apostolic letter "The Coming of the Third Millennium," that acknowledging the weaknesses of the past is an act of honesty and courage. It helps to strengthen our faith, and it helps us to face today's temptations (# 33). But we should also forget and forgive the wrong done to us. We should share in God's and in Jesus' mercy.

Prayer Jesus Christ, light that never fades, dispel the mists all around us, teach us your mercy, and give us your unfailing gentleness at all times. Amen.

Practice Tell your children or a friend a story about forgiveness and reconciliation today, preferably one in which you yourself either offered forgiveness or were forgiven.

The People of God

"Which of the two did the father's will?" (Mt 21:31).

The father asked his two sons to go and work in his vineyard. The elder one said "no," but went after all, and the younger one said "yes," but did not go. "Which of the two did the father's will?" The answer is simple, and it should be the criterion we use to judge ourselves and the people around us.

Since the Second Vatican Council we have grown accustomed to calling ourselves "the people of God." The temptation is to use this term for the baptized only, a custom that declares "outsiders" as not belonging to the family of God. Would that be the right conclusion?

Jesus uses another standard when speaking about the family of God. The ones who belong to that family are those who recognize true righteousness and who are willing to live up to it.

It is not the group you belong to that counts. It is what you are willing to do that makes the difference. Sinners might feel the need for a greater righteousness in our world better than others do. And though saying "no" for now, they might be the ones who are better inclined to work at doing something about our wronged world than those who do not feel its pain.

PRAYER Lord, may your kingdom come! May our works of penance and preparation for your birth please you, and may we be ready for your reign which is so near. Amen.

PRACTICE Pray the "Our Father" slowly and reflectively today. Think about the phrase "your kingdom come." Praying these words means that you are saying "yes" to the reign of God, but will this be followed by a "yes" in your actions today?

Genesis 49:2, 8–10; Psalm 72:3–4, 7–8; 17; Matthew 1:1–17

Sacred Numbers

"Fourteen..., fourteen..., fourteen... to Christ." (Mt 1:17).

It is sometimes said that people today do not attach the same importance to numbers as our ancestors did. We do pay attention to numbers, of course. Just think about the Dow Jones and the Nasdaq numbers that are announced at the end of each news broadcast.

Our interest in numbers is different from the old fascination. We no longer attribute to numbers a secret and sacred meaning, as Matthew did in his gospel when he divided the human history since Abraham into three periods of fourteen generations. For him, those numbers meant that the end had come. It meant for him that the last era of this world had begun: the fullness of time.

Pope John Paul definitely still believes in this kind of mysticism. He wrote (in his document on the third millennium), "the fact that in the fullness of time the Eternal Word took on the condition of a creature gives a unique cosmic value to the event that took place in Bethlehem two thousand years ago" (#3).

The pope invites us to prepare ourselves for a celebration of this jubilee, by renewing our hope in the definitive coming of the kingdom of God, preparing daily for it in our hearts, in the Christian community to which we belong, in our particular social context, and in the world itself (#46).

Prayer Jesus Christ, you are the joy and happiness of all who are waiting for your coming. You are the realization of God's peace and justice among us. Come to us and do not delay. Amen.

Practice Find out about how your particular parish or diocese is preparing for Jubilee Year 2000. How can you tap into these preparations? How can you begin preparing today?

Jeremiah 23:5–8; Psalm 72:1, 12–13, 18–19; Matthew 1:18–24

Sharing Mary's Hope

"She was found to be with child" (Mt 1:18).

According to Matthew's account today an angel had to intervene to save Mary from Joseph's decision to divorce her. Joseph had already made up his mind to do so when "the angel of the Lord appeared to him in a dream" (Mt 1:20). And though "he took his wife to his home," Mary's problems can't have been over. She had to cope with an unexpected child, her husband, the rest of her family, further relations, and all kinds of authorities who pushed her around.

She must have been a practical, down-to-earth woman who made the ordinary extraordinary and grace-filled. She is our model of how to love God and our neighbor.

When Mary explains herself to her kinswoman Elizabeth— whom she went to help—not only does she sing her love for God, she also declares her concern for her poor and hungry neighbors. She expresses fully the longing of the poor for a more just and charitable world. No wonder that she remains such a controversial figure in the world. She keeps on challenging us year after year after year.

Prayer Let us pray with joyfilled hearts to Jesus Christ, born of the woman Mary! Jesus, give us new life by your coming, and renew us please by the coming anniversary of your birth. Amen.

Practice Read Mary's prayer of praise, called the Magnificat, which is in Luke's Gospel (1:46–55). See whether you can make its words your own plan of action!

Judges 13:2–7, 24–25; Psalm 71:3–6, 16–17; Luke 1:5–25

God Intervenes

"Elizabeth was barren" (Lk 1:7).

The readings today tell the same story about two women. They were both barren. One was the mother of Samson. Her name is not even mentioned, though we are told that God sent an angel to her! The other woman is Elizabeth, the mother of John the Baptizer. She tells us that the villagers humiliated her because she was childless. In the lives of both women God intervenes, taking what the world considered worthless to show God's glory. In sacred Scripture God often intervenes in this way.

Consider too that our creator did not use gold, uranium, diamonds, or pearls when making the human body, but just dust. God did not speak to Moses from a mighty cedar, but from a low growing bush. God picked David to be king, though David's father had not even bothered to call his son from the field.

Jesus followed the same divine pattern when working his miracles. Consider, for example, how the loaves and fishes were multiplied to feed a crowd of thousands!

However humble and domestic our life stories might be, we are deeply valued in the eyes of our maker, created as we are in God's image. All of us have our own role to play in God's mighty work.

Prayer Jesus, my love and my life, you took our weakness upon yourself; fill us with the strength of your own divine life. Show those who feel humbled and downtrodden the glory of your divine presence. Amen.

Practice Take time today to quietly reflect upon the positive role you have played in the lives of your family, your community, and your world. Thank God for letting you be an instrument in all these ways.

You Are Special

"Rejoice, so highly favored! The Lord is with you!" (Lk 1:28).

The woman received a beautiful string of pearls in the mail. She could guess who had sent this gift, but she almost burst into tears when she did not find any message with the gift. She went through the package three times, but there was no note, no word attached, only those pearls. What she really wanted was a card that said "I love you!" That message would have been more valuable to her than the most expensive gift.

When the archangel from God greets Mary in Luke's gospel, the first thing Mary hears is: "Rejoice, you are special, precious. You are loved!" God does not leave out the important words. All further blessings in Mary's life followed from that greeting.

Still today, words of affirmation and love are blessings for us. They are the kind of words that bring people together. They make the connections needed to turn this world into a civilization of love! Still today, God greets us as Mary was greeted. Each one of us is unique, precious, and loved in God's eyes. Each one of us has a special role to play! God calls each one of us by name.

Prayer Jesus, light of the world, ignite in our hearts the flame of your love. May our hearts be on fire to do God's will, just as Mary's was. Mother Mary, blessed virgin, pray for us. Amen.

Practice Pay attention to your greetings today! Greet someone that you would not normally have greeted. Watch his or her pleasant surprise. Do your part today to knit the world around you in kindness and love.

Micah 5:1–4; Psalm 80:2–3, 15–16, 18–19; Hebrews 10:5–10; Luke 1:39–45

Jesus Brings Peace

"He himself will be peace" (Mi 5:4).

The prophet Micah describes the messianic hopes of the people of his time. He put it all together in these few words: "He himself will be peace."

It is a hope that has not changed over the years. In 1983 a leading pollster conducted an extensive poll in the United States. Questionnaires were distributed to people of various ages and occupations. The key question was: "What are you looking for most in life?" When the results were compiled the analysts were surprised. Most of them had expected answers that would reflect materialistic goals, but the top three things that people wanted were love, joy, and peace—the first three fruits of the Spirit.

The world will have no peace until all the nations are at peace. The nations will have no peace until the families in them are at peace. And families will enjoy no peace until their members are at peace.

Micah prophesies that Jesus will be peace! It is what the angels sang: "Peace on earth!" It is this peace we should welcome as the beginning of the overall peace and justice of God's kingdom.

Prayer   Jesus, who revealed your glory to the world when you were born in Bethlehem, free us from all sin and guilt when you come again in glory. Amen.

Practice   Jesus paid a price for being "peace." He willingly paid this price so that we too would have peace. Join in his struggle by contributing to peace in your world today, at least in some small way.

1 Samuel 1:24–28; 1 Samuel 2:1, 4–8; Luke 1:46–56

Mary's Option

"God has exalted the lowly and filled the hungry" (Lk 1:52–53).

Every day of the year the church sings the Magnificat in its evening prayer. This song reveals and expresses Mary's choices and intentions. Justice is going to be done to the lowly and the poor. It is a melody taken up by Jesus when he tells the crowds around him that he came "to preach the good news to the poor" (Mt 11:5; Lk 7:22).

In his apostolic letter, "The Coming of the Third Millennium," Pope John Paul asks us to join the chorus: "How can we fail to lay greater emphasis on the church's preferential option for the poor and the outcast?" (#51).

He has a specific proposal: "Christians will have to raise their voices on behalf of all the poor in the world, to give thought among other things, to reducing substantially, if not canceling outright, the international debt which seriously threatens the future of many nations" (Ibid).

The problem with such an admonition is that it comes from outside us, from above. If we were more aware of Jesus' Spirit within us, we too would be concerned about the poor and the outcast deep within our own hearts. Wasn't Mary's option for the poor based on the presence of that Spirit in her? The same can be true of us.

Prayer Come, Jesus, come! Do not let us become estranged either from you or from one another. Enable us to live in your goodness. We ask you this through the intercession of your blessed Mother Mary. Amen.

Practice Give some thought today to the huge debt that many poor countries face. Are you willing to have our government forgive these debts? This would be Mary's option!

Fourth Tuesday in Advent
Malachi 3:1–4, 23–24; Psalm 25:4–5, 8–10, 14; Luke 1:57–66

The Power of Speech

"His power of speech returned and he praised God" (Lk 1:64).

The President of the Theological Union recently presented a gift to the school's receptionist. He said that the first contact with this establishment is through her, and that she is really its ambassador. He might have added something else, something which applies to all of us; that is, speaking to and with others is something divine!

To be able to express our thoughts and emotions is part of being created in the "image of God." The book of Genesis tells us that God said: "Let there be light," and there was light. God pronounced the names "Adam" and "Eve" and they stood before God in all their glory.

At Christmas we celebrate how God's Word is born among us. This emphasis on the "Word" teaches us that our words and gestures are also meant to communicate God's Word. We do this when our words offer life, joy, comfort, consolation, and peace to others. The lesson of Advent and Christmas is this: our words should always echo God's Word and Spirit! We are ambassadors for Christ.

Prayer To our redeemer who came to bring good news to the poor, let us pray. May we see your glory, Jesus, and may we be your instruments through all our words and deeds. Amen.

Practice Today really listen to someone who wants to tell you something and then answer carefully and appropriately. Whether the one you listen to is a friend, your partner, your colleague, or your child, listen with your heart—as Jesus listened.